MW01628083

The Girls' Cookbook

A collection of recipes that are perfect for your little chef!

First published in 2011
LOVE FOOD is an imprint of Parragon Books Ltd

Parragon
Queen Street House
4 Queen Street
Bath BA1 1HE, UK

ISBN: 978-1-4454-3803-0

Printed in China

Design by Talking Design
New photography by Mike Cooper
New home economy by Lincoln Jefferson
New recipes by Rachel Carter
Introduction by Moira Butterfield

With a special thank you to Isabelle and Eloïse Merry.

Notes for the Reader
This book uses metric, imperial, and US standard measurements. Follow the same units of measurement throughout; do not mix metric and imperial. All spoon measurements are level: teaspoons are assumed to be 5 ml, and tablespoons are assumed to be 15 ml. Unless otherwise stated, milk is assumed to be whole, eggs are large, and individual vegetables are medium. Pepper is freshly ground black pepper.

The times given are an approximate guide only. Preparation times differ according to the techniques used by different people and the cooking times may also vary from those given. Optional ingredients, variations, or serving suggestions have not been included in the calculations.

Recipes using raw or very lightly cooked eggs should be avoided by infants, the elderly, pregnant women, convalescents, and anyone with a chronic illness. Pregnant and breast-feeding women are advised to avoid eating peanuts and peanut products. People with nut allergies should be aware that some of the prepared ingredients used in the recipes in this book may contain nuts. Always check the packaging before use.

Picture Acknowledgments:
The publisher would like to thank the following for permission to reproduce copyright material on the front cover: Two girls (3-5) having tea party, one dipping waffle in candy © Luca Trovato/Getty Images

Contents

Steps to yummy cooking

There are three magic secrets to cooking:

Cooking is a lot of fun.

Cooking makes people happy.

Cooking is a great way to be creative.

Those are pretty powerful secrets, don't you think?

You'll have a great time trying out recipes. Your friends and family will love sharing the treats you make, and healthy food is good for everybody.

Get set:

Ask the adults in your home if it's okay to cook. These recipes are designed to be made together so you will need their help with difficult bits. Show them the recipe you want to try and ask them to explain any words or steps that you don't understand.

Read the recipe carefully. Before you start, you'll need to make sure you have all the right ingredients and the equipment you need.

Always wash your hands before you start. That way you won't pass on any dirt or germs in your food.

Wear an apron to keep your clothes clean. You'll want to put yummy food in your mouth, not down your front!

All about ovens:

You might need to warm up an oven for your cooking. This is known as preheating the oven. Ask an adult to help you do this.

Ovens measure heat in Fahrenheit (°F), though some ovens in other countries use Celsius (°C).

Both heat measurements are in this book, so choose the one that's right for your oven.

Measure it:

You'll need to measure your ingredients carefully, so that your food will cook correctly and taste good.

Use a large measuring cup to measure liquids. Look at eyelevel so you can properly read the measurements on the cup.

Use a standard set of measuring cups for dry ingredients, such as sugar. The set of cups come in ¼ cup, ⅓ cup, ½ cup, and 1 cup sizes. To use a measuring cup, you need to level the ingredients—unless the recipe says it should be heaping, which means to let it go a little above the cup. To level the ingredient, push the straight edge of a spatula across the top edge of the cup.

Know your spoons:

The best spoons to use for measuring are a standard set of measuring spoons.

A teaspoon (tsp) is one of the smaller spoons, about the same size you might use to stir a drink.

A tablespoon (tbsp) is one of the biggest spoons—a little bit too big to eat with but perfect for cooking.

If a recipe says "one teaspoon" or "one tablespoon" it means a level spoonful, not a heaping spoonful. Level it as you would for a measuring cup.

Cook's rules:

Always use oven mitts if you need to pick up a hot dish or a pan. That way you won't burn your hands.

Make sure you don't leave a mess after you have finished. If you clean up, the chances are you'll get to cook again soon.

How to use this book:

If you see this symbol (!), it means you need to ask an adult for help. This could be because a hot oven, stove top, electrical appliance, sharp knives, or scissors are involved in the recipe preparation.

All the recipes have symbols to help you. Look out for:

Serves/Makes

Preparation time (in minutes)

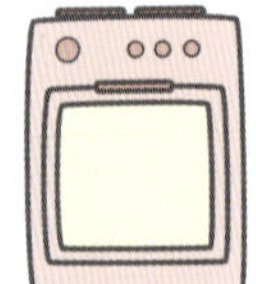
Cooking time (in minutes)

After you have made a recipe, you can grade your success, 1–10, by using the heart that looks like this:

Follow the fairy's dotted path on the oppostite page to check you are ready to start cooking …

Now you're ready to cook something yummy!

Know your equipment

1. Saucepan
2. Frying pan
3. Oven mitts
4. Cutting board
5. Mixing bowl
6. Rolling pin
7. Cooling rack
8. Balloon whisk
9. Baking pans
10. Wooden spoon
11. Measuring cups
12. Spatula
13. Muffin tray
14. Measuring cup
15. Scales
16. Strainer
17. Cookie cutter
18. Grater
19. Knife

14
15
18
11
16
6
13
5
7
8

Bake the most delicious treats

Butterfly Cakes

Bubbly Pink Cupcakes

Strawberry Muffins

Chocolate Chip Cookies

Fairy Wands

Button Cookies

Butterfly Cakes

The little butterfly wings look really pretty and you can have a lot of fun decorating them with sprinkles.

10

What you need:

⅔ cup unsalted butter, cut into small pieces, softened

¾ cup superfine sugar

½ tsp vanilla extract

2 extra-large eggs, lightly beaten

heaping 1 cup self-rising flour, sifted

1–2 tbsp milk

sprinkles, to decorate

Buttercream:

6 tbsp unsalted butter, softened

heaping 1⅓ cups confectioners' sugar

1 tbsp orange juice

1. Preheat the oven to 350°F/180°C. Line a muffin pan with 12 cupcake liners.

2. Put the butter and sugar into a large bowl and beat, using an electric handheld mixer, until the mixture is pale and fluffy. Add the vanilla extract and 1 egg and beat on a low speed.

3. Beat in a tablespoonful of flour, then the second egg and the milk. Fold in the rest of the flour, using a wooden spoon, to make a smooth mixture.

4. Using a tablespoon, spoon the same amount of mixture into each cupcake liner. Bake for 12–15 minutes, until risen and golden. Remove from the oven and let the cupcakes cool a little, then move to a wire rack.

5. When cool, slice off the top of each cupcake and cut in half to make 2 wings. For the buttercream, beat together the butter, confectioners' sugar, and orange juice in a medium bowl. Add a drop of the pink food coloring at a time until you get the right shade of pale pink.

6. Place a spoonful of buttercream on top of each cupcake and decorate with sprinkles. Place the wings on top.

Step 2

Step 4

Step 6

Bubbly Pink Cupcakes

These cute cupcakes look just like glasses of pink ice cream sodas. Add a straw to the top and serve as a fun treat!

10

What you need:

1 cup self-rising flour, sifted
¼ tsp baking powder
½ cup unsalted butter, cut into small pieces, softened
heaping ½ cup superfine sugar
2 extra-large eggs, lightly beaten
pink, white, and red sprinkles, to decorate
10 pink drinking straws, cut to 3-inches/8-cm long, to serve

Buttercream:

½ cup unsalted butter, softened
1¾ cups confectioners' sugar
1 tbsp lemon juice
pink food coloring

1. Preheat the oven to 350°F/180°C. Line a muffin pan with 10 cupcake liners.

2. Put the flour and baking powder into a large bowl. Add the butter, superfine sugar, and eggs and beat, using an electric handheld mixer, until the mixture is pale and fluffy.

3. Using a tablespoon, spoon the same amount of mixture into each cupcake liner. Bake for 15–20 minutes, until risen and golden. Remove from the oven and let the cupcakes cool a little, then move to a cooling rack.

4. For the buttercream, beat together the butter, confectioners' sugar, and lemon juice in a medium bowl. Stir in a little pink food coloring to make a pale pink color.

5. Thickly swirl the buttercream over the tops of the cupcakes using a palette knife. Put the sprinkles on a plate, hold onto the paper liners, and roll the cupcake edges in the sprinkles.

6. Push a straw into the top of the cupcakes to decorate.

Strawberry Muffins

It's not until you bite into these delicious muffins that you discover the secret strawberry jelly filling inside.

10

What you need:

1¾ cups all-purpose flour
1 tsp baking powder
¾ cup superfine sugar
½ cup milk
2 extra-large eggs
⅔ cup unsalted butter, melted
12 tsp strawberry jelly
6 strawberries, halved, to decorate

Buttercream:

3 tbsp unsalted butter, softened
⅔ cup confectioners' sugar
½ tsp vanilla extract
1–2 tsp milk

(!) 1. Preheat the oven to 400°F/200°C. Line a muffin pan with 12 baking cups.

2. Sift the flour and baking powder into a large bowl. Stir in the superfine sugar, using a wooden spoon. Put the milk, eggs, and melted butter in a pitcher and beat together with a whisk. Pour a little at a time into the bowl, stirring gently until combined.

3. Spoon a tablespoon of the muffin mixture into each baking cup, then add a teaspoonful of jelly. Top the jelly with the rest of the muffin mixture.

(!) 4. Bake in the preheated oven for 20–25 minutes, until risen and golden. Remove the muffins from the oven and let cool a little, then move to a cooling rack.

5. For the buttercream, beat together the butter, confectioners' sugar, vanilla extract, and milk in a medium bowl.

6. Place a spoonful of the buttercream on top of each muffin, then decorate with a strawberry half.

Step 2

Step 4

Step 6

Chocolate Chip Cookies

These yummy chocolate chip cookies taste best warm. They are so delicious you'll want to make them time and time again!

/10

What you need:

heaping ½ cup unsalted butter, softened and cut into small pieces

½ cup brown sugar

2 tbsp light corn syrup

1 tsp vanilla extract

1 cup all-purpose flour

pinch of salt

6 oz/175 g milk chocolate, cut into small chunks

1 egg, beaten

1. Preheat the oven to 350°F/180°C. Line two baking sheets with parchment paper.

2. Place the butter and brown sugar in a large bowl and, using a wooden spoon, beat until mixed together.

3. Add the corn syrup and vanilla extract and stir again until combined. Stir in the flour, salt, chocolate, and egg and gently mix together to make a soft dough.

4. Spoon small amounts of the dough onto the baking sheets, making sure you space them well apart, and bake in the preheated oven for 12–15 minutes, until golden brown.

5. Remove the baking sheets from the oven and let the cookies cool a little, then move to a cooling rack to cool completely.

Step 2

Step 3

Step 4

Fairy Wands

Add a little magic to your cooking with these fantastic fairy wands. You can decorate them to make each wand special!

10

What you need:

2 cups all-purpose flour, sifted, plus extra for dusting

½ cup superfine sugar

½ cup cold butter, cut into small pieces

1 tbsp milk

12 wooden craft sticks

To decorate

1 egg white, lightly beaten

pink pearl sugar balls

pink edible glitter

(!) 1. Preheat the oven to 325°F/160°C. Line 2 baking sheets with parchment paper.

2. Put the flour and sugar in a large bowl and mix together. Rub in the butter, using your fingertips, to make a soft buttery mixture.

3. Stir in the milk, using a wooden spoon, then bring the mixture together with your hands to make a dough.

4. Lightly flour the work surface and rolling pin. Knead the dough gently until smooth, then roll out until it is about ¼ inch/5 mm thick. Use a heart-shape cutter to stamp out 12 hearts and carefully put on the prepared baking sheets.

5. Press a small, wooden ice-cream stick into each one and cover the wooden "handles" with aluminum foil so that they don't burn while baking in the oven.

(!) 6. Bake in the preheated oven for 15–20 minutes, until golden brown. Remove from the oven and let the cookies cool a little, then move to a cooling rack.

7. Brush the hearts with egg white, sprinkle the decorations of your choice over them, and let them cool.

Button Cookies

These button-shape cookies can be threaded with colored ribbons to make them look extra special.

10

What you need:

2 cups all-purpose flour, sifted, plus extra for dusting

heaping 2 tbsp cornstarch

⅓ cup superfine sugar

¾ cup unsalted butter cut into small pieces

1–2 tsp milk

thin ribbons, to decorate

1. Preheat the oven to 350°F/180°C. Line 2 baking sheets with parchment paper.

2. Put the flour, cornstarch, and superfine sugar in a large bowl. Rub in the butter, using your fingertips, to make a soft buttery mixture.

3. Stir in the milk, using a wooden spoon, then bring the mixture together with your hands to make a dough.

4. Lightly flour the work surface and rolling pin. Gently knead the dough until smooth, then roll out until it is about ¼ inch/5 mm thick.

5. Use a round cutter to stamp out 19 circles and carefully put on the prepared baking sheets.

6. Use a toothpick to make 4 holes in each cookie so it looks like a button, turning the toothpick to make the holes big enough to thread the ribbon through.

7. Bake in the preheated oven for 10–12 minutes, until pale and golden. Remove from the oven and let the cookies cool a little, then move to a cooling rack. When cool, thread the ribbons through the holes and tie the ends into a bow.

Step 2

Step 4

Step 6

Impress with everyday eats

Very Berry Pancakes

Perfect Oatmeal

Veggie Skewers

Super Stuffed Potatoes

Mighty Meatballs

Fantastic Fajitas

Very Berry Pancakes

Your family and friends will love these light pancakes—they're so delicious that they'll disappear in seconds!

10

What you need:

1¼ cups self-rising flour, sifted

2 tbsp superfine sugar

1 extra-large egg, lightly beaten

¾ cup milk

3 tbsp thick plain yogurt, plus extra to serve

2 tbsp unsalted butter, for frying

2½ cups frozen mixed berries, such as raspberries, blackberries, and blueberries, defrosted

maple syrup, to serve

1. Put the flour and sugar in a mixing bowl and stir until mixed together. Make a dip in the center.

2. Mix together the egg and milk in a pitcher. Pour the milk mixture into the flour. Add the yogurt and stir with a wooden spoon until you have a smooth batter.

3. Melt ½ tablespoon of the butter in a skillet. Add 3 tablespoonfuls of batter to make 3 pancakes, about 2½ inches/6 cm in diameter.

4. Cook for 2 minutes, until bubbles appear on the top and the underneath is golden brown. Flip each pancake over with a spatula and cook for another minute.

5. Repeat with the rest of the batter to make about 16 pancakes. Add a little more butter when the skillet looks dry.

6. Serve the pancakes with a large spoonful of fruit and yogurt and drizzle over the maple syrup.

Step 1

Step 3

Step 6

Perfect Oatmeal

Just the thing to warm you up on a cold winter's morning, this creamy oatmeal is topped with a cinnamon applesauce, maple syrup, and pecans.

10

What you need:

2¼ cups whole rolled oats
3½ cups milk
3½ cups water
8 pecans, to serve (optional)
maple syrup, to serve

Cinnamon applesauce:

4 firm apples (Granny Smith, or any good cooking apple)
1 tsp lemon juice
¾ cup water
½–1 tsp ground cinnamon

1. For the applesauce, remove the skin from the apples, using a vegetable peeler. Cut the apple into quarters, remove the core, then cut into small pieces.

2. Put the apples, lemon juice, water, and cinnamon in a small saucepan. Cover and simmer for 15 minutes, until the apples are soft.

3. While the apple mixture is cooking, put the oats in a large saucepan with the milk and water and bring to a boil.

4. When the oat mixture is bubbling, reduce the heat to low, cover the pan halfway with a lid, and simmer for 8 minutes, stirring frequently.

5. Mash the apple with a fork until mushy. Spoon the creamy oatmeal into 4 bowls, then top each one with applesauce.

6. Add the pecans, if using, and drizzle over the maple syrup. Arrange the nuts and syrup in a fun pattern.

Veggie Skewers

Use brightly colored vegetables to create vibrant veggie skewers! These skewers are so yummy that they'll brighten up any day.

10

What you need:

1 yellow and 1 red pepper, seeded and cut into small chunks

1 zucchini, peeled and sliced

1½ cups cleaned and halved button mushrooms

barbecue sauce (store bought), to serve

Flavored oil:

2 tbsp olive oil

1 tbsp honey

1 tbsp ketchup

1 clove garlic, crushed

½ tsp dried mixed herbs

salt and pepper

1. For the flavored oil, put the oil, honey, ketchup, garlic, herbs, and salt and pepper into a small bowl and mix together.

2. Place the vegetables in a clean plastic food bag and pour in the flavored oil. Seal the bag and turn it a few times to coat all the vegetables in the oil. Let stand for 10 minutes.

(!) 3. Thread the vegetables onto 8 skewers, alternating the different colors.

(!) 4. Turn the broiler to high. Add the skewers and cook for 8–10 minutes, turning regularly, until the vegetables are starting to soften.

5. Serve the skewers with the barbecue sauce.

Step 2

Step 3

Step 4

Super Stuffed Potatoes

These warm cheesy potatoes are the perfect treat for a delicious meal. Serve them on their own or with some tasty fresh vegetables.

/10

What you need:

4 medium baking potatoes, cleaned

1 tbsp olive oil

1⅓ cups grated cheddar cheese

2 tbsp butter

3 tbsp milk

1 cup chopped ham

salt and pepper

1. Preheat the oven to 425°F/220°C. Rub the potato skins with the olive oil, using a piece of clean paper towel. Sprinkle the skins with a little salt.

2. Place the potatoes on a baking sheet, pierce them with a fork, and bake in the preheated oven for 1 hour or until the potatoes are soft when pierced with the tip of a sharp knife.

3. Remove the potatoes from the oven, cut in half, and let cool for 10–15 minutes.

4. Carefully scoop out the potato flesh, without breaking the skins, put the potato into a mixing bowl, and mash well with a fork.

5. Add 1 cup of the cheese, the butter, milk, and ham and season with some salt and pepper.

6. Put the potato mixture back into the skins using a spoon and top with the remaining cheese. Place on a baking sheet and put back in the oven for 10–15 minutes, until the tops are golden brown.

Step 1

Step 4

Step 6

Mighty Meatballs

Everyone loves meatballs and these are no exception. They come in a rich tomato sauce and are served on a bed of swirly spaghetti.

/10

1. Put the bread in a food processor and process until it makes breadcrumbs. Add the ground beef, garlic, egg, Parmesan cheese, and salt and pepper.

2. Process the meat mixture until it comes together in a ball. Flour your hands, take small amounts of the mixture, and roll into balls the size of walnuts. Let chill in the refrigerator.

3. For the tomato sauce, heat the oil in a saucepan and add the garlic and oregano. Stir for 1 minute.

4. Add the chopped tomatoes, tomato paste, and sugar. Bring to a boil, then reduce the heat and simmer for 8 minutes.

5. Carefully place the meatballs in the pan and spoon the sauce over them. Cover and simmer for 20 minutes, turning the meatballs occasionally.

6. Meanwhile, cook the spaghetti in a large pan of salted water, following the directions on the package. Drain and serve with the meatballs and sauce.

What you need:

1½ slices crustless, day-old bread, broken into chunks

14 oz/400 g lean ground beef

2 cloves garlic, crushed

1 extra-large egg, lightly beaten

heaping ⅓ cup finely grated Parmesan cheese

flour, for coating

10 oz/300 g dried spaghetti

salt and pepper

Tomato sauce:

2 tbsp olive oil

2 cloves garlic, crushed

2 tsp dried oregano

3½ cups canned chopped tomatoes

1 tbsp tomato paste

1 tsp sugar

Fantastic Fajitas

Once you've made your delicious chicken, you can have fun making the fajitas. Make sure you wrap them tightly, because you don't want your veggies falling out.

/10

* plus marinating time

What you need:

grated zest and juice 1 lime
1 tsp sugar
1 tsp dried oregano
2 tsp smoked paprika
2 tbsp olive oil
3 chicken breasts, cut into bite size pieces
1 red onion, finely sliced
1 orange and 1 red pepper, seeded and diced
1 cups wiped and sliced button mushrooms

To serve:

8 tortilla wraps
grated cheddar cheese
guacamole and sour cream
shredded iceberg lettuce

1. Put the lime zest and juice, sugar, oregano, paprika, and half of the olive oil in a large bowl and mix together.

2. Add the chicken and toss well to coat. Cover with plastic wrap and place in the refrigerator for 1–2 hours.

3. Heat the remaining oil in a large skillet and cook the marinated chicken for 4–5 minutes. Add the vegetables and continue to stir fry for a further 3–4 minutes, stirring regularly, until the chicken is thoroughly cooked.

4. Heat a nonstick skillet or grill pan, then add the tortillas, one at a time, and warm for 10 seconds on each side.

5. Serve each wrap with a spoonful of the chicken mixture, topped with a little cheese, guacamole, sour cream, and lettuce, and wrap up tightly.

Step 1

Step 2

Step 5

Throw the most perfect party

Golden Nuggets

Pizza Party

Cute Mini Burgers

Hot Dogs & Fries

Maple Syrup Popcorn

Scrumptious S'mores

Golden Nuggets

These golden nuggets of breadcrumbs and chicken taste great and are delicious when dipped into ketchup or mustard.

10

What you need:

¼ cup all-purpose flour

2 eggs, beaten

¼ cup grated cheddar cheese

3 cups fresh breadcrumbs

4 chicken breasts, chopped into chunks

salt and pepper

ketchup and mustard, to serve

(!) 1. Preheat the oven to 400°F/200°C. Line a baking sheet with parchment paper.

2. Put the flour in a small bowl and season with some salt and pepper. Put the eggs in another small bowl, then put the cheese and breadcrumbs in a third small bowl.

3. Dip each chicken chunk first in the flour to coat lightly, then dip in the egg, and finally in the breadcrumb mixture.

(!) 4. Place the chicken chunks on the prepared baking sheet and cook for 22–25 minutes, turning once until the coating is golden brown and the chicken is cooked through.

5. Serve immediately with ketchup and mustard.

Step 2

Step 3

Step 4

Pizza Party

This makes 2 pizzas—perfect for a party! Each quarter of the pizza has a different topping, which means that there is something for everyone.

/10

* plus time for crusts to stand

What you need:

3 cups white bread flour, plus extra for dusting

1 tsp salt

7 g sachet active dry yeast

1 tbsp olive oil, plus extra for brushing

1 cup lukewarm water

10 oz/300 g fresh mozzarella balls, torn into pieces

sliced pitted black olives, ham slices, pineapple chunks, variety of sliced vegetables, for the topping

Tomato sauce:

1 tbsp olive oil

scant 1 cup tomato puree

2 tsp tomato paste

1 tsp dried oregano

1. Mix together the flour, salt, and yeast in a large bowl. Make a well in the center and pour in the oil and water, then mix to make a soft dough.

2. Lightly flour the work surface and rolling pin, then knead the dough for 10 minutes, until smooth.

(!) 3. Divide the dough into 2 pieces and roll out to make 2 thin pizza crusts. Put the pizza crusts on 2 baking sheets and let stand in a warm place for 20 minutes. Preheat the oven to 450°F/230°C.

4. To make the tomato sauce, mix together the oil, tomato puree, tomato paste, and oregano in a small bowl. Spoon it onto the crusts and spread thinly with the back of a tablespoon.

5. Sprinkle the pizzas with the mozzarella and top each quarter with a different topping of your choice.

(!) 6. Brush the topping with oil and bake the pizzas for 10–15 minutes. Remove from the oven, then cut each pizza into 8 slices with a knife or pizza cutter.

Step 1

Step 3

Step 5

Cute Mini Burgers

Making your own hamburgers is a lot of fun and they taste great! These mini burgers are so cute that everyone at your party will love them!

10

What you need:

1 onion, finely grated
2 cloves garlic, crushed
1 lb/450 g ground beef
1 tbsp Cajun seasoning
2 tbsp ketchup
1 tbsp olive oil
12 slices Swiss cheese
salt and pepper

To serve:

mini burger buns
pickles, thinly sliced
lettuce
ketchup

1. Put the onion, garlic, ground beef, Cajun seasoning, ketchup, and salt and pepper in a large bowl and mix together with your hands until well combined.

2. Make into 12 equal small patties.

3. (!) Heat half of the oil in a large skillet and cook the first 6 burgers for 4–5 minutes. Turn the burgers and cook for 2–3 minutes, then top with a slice of cheese and continue cooking for another 2–3 minutes or until the cheese is just starting to melt.

4. (!) Check that the hamburgers are thoroughly cooked by piercing with the tip of a knife. Any juices that run out should be clear. Repeat the cooking process with the remaining oil and hamburgers.

5. (!) Serve the burgers in the buns, topped with the pickles, lettuce, and ketchup. Secure with a toothpick and serve.

Step 1

Step 2

Step 5

Hot Dogs & Fries

These mini hot dogs make great party food, and the fries are extra special because they are homemade sweet potato fries.

10

What you need:

4 sweet potatoes, peeled and cut into thin fries

2 tbsp olive oil

4 all beef hot dogs, cut in half

salt and pepper

4 large hot dogs buns and ketchup, to serve

1. Preheat the oven to 400°F/ 200°C. Line a baking sheet with parchment paper.

2. Put the sweet potato fries on the prepared baking sheet.

3. Drizzle over the oil and add some salt and pepper. Use your hands to coat the fries in the oil.

4. Place the sweet potatoes in the preheated oven for 20–25 minutes, until they are golden brown, turning occasionally.

5. Meanwhile, cook the hot dogs following the package directions.

6. Cut each hot dog bun in half and place in a bun with some ketchup. Serve with the sweet potato fries.

Step 2

Step 3

Step 6

Maple Syrup Popcorn

Both fun to make and very tasty to eat, popcorn is the perfect party snack. Serve it in a big bowl so everyone can share!

10

What you need:

1–2 tbsp vegetable oil
⅔ cup popping corn
1 tbsp butter
3 tbsp maple syrup

1. Pour the oil into a saucepan and heat over medium heat.

2. Carefully add the popcorn to the pan in an even layer and cover with a lid. A glass lid is best so you can see into the pan.

3. Cook the popcorn over medium–low heat, shaking the pan occasionally, until only a few of the corn kernels are popping.

4. Pour the popcorn into a large mixing bowl, discarding any kernels that may not have popped.

5. Melt the butter in a small saucepan, then pour in the maple syrup. Bring to a boil, then remove from the heat and cool.

6. Pour the maple syrup sauce over the popcorn and stir to mix together.

Scrumptious S'mores

Make really delicious s'mores by sandwiching chocolate and marshmallows between two chocolate chip cookies.

10

What you need:

8 large store-bought chocolate chip cookies

8 marshmallows, sliced in half horizontally (or you could use mini marshmallows)

2 oz/55 g milk chocolate, cut into small squares

1. Preheat the oven to 400°F/200°C. Line a baking sheet with parchment paper.

2. Place four cookies on the prepared baking sheet upside down and top with 4 pieces of marshmallow and a few pieces of chocolate.

3. Place another cookie, right-side up, on top and press down lightly.

4. Place in the preheated oven for 6–8 minutes, until the marshmallow is starting to ooze and the chocolate is beginning to melt.

5. Put the s'mores on a pretty plate and serve warm.

Step 2

Step 3

Step 5

Make the yummiest desserts

Chocolate Mousse

Ice Cream Sundae

Meringue Clouds

My Own Apple Pie

Raspberry Parfaits

Chocolate Mousse

Nothing could be more delicious to eat than chocolate mousse. Top with cream and pretty sprinkles.

/10

What you need:

⅔ cup light cream

5 oz/140 g milk chocolate, coarsely chopped

2 tbsp unsalted butter, cut into small pieces

To decorate:

heavy cream

pink sprinkles

1. Put the light cream in a small saucepan over medium heat and slowly bring to boiling point.
2. Add the chocolate and butter and reduce the heat to low. Stir continually until the chocolate and butter have melted and the mixture is smooth.
3. Pour the mixture into 4 teacups or ramekins and place in the refrigerator to set for about 30 minutes.
4. When the desserts have set, spoon a little of the heavy cream over the top of each one and decorate with some pink sprinkles.

Step 1

Step 2

Step 4

Ice Cream Sundae

There's only one way to describe this sundae—delicious! It's so good it would make a great birthday treat.

/10

What you need:

¼ cup chopped mixed nuts (optional)

8 scoops of vanilla ice cream

grated chocolate and marshmallows, to serve

Strawberry sauce:

9 oz/250 g strawberries, cut in half with stems removed

2 tbsp freshly squeezed orange juice

2 tbsp superfine sugar

(!) 1. Put the chopped nuts in a dry skillet and heat for 3 minutes, until slightly toasted (if using). Let cool.

(!) 2. For the strawberry sauce, put the strawberries in a blender with the orange juice and process until smooth.

(!) 3. Transfer the mixture to a saucepan and add the sugar. Cook over medium heat for 10–12 minutes, or until thickened. Let cool.

4. Put a spoonful of the strawberry sauce in the bottom of a tall glass. Add two scoops of ice cream and another spoonful of strawberry sauce. Repeat to make 4 sundaes.

5. Sprinkle with the nuts and chocolate. Arrange the marshmallows on top. Serve immediately.

Meringue Clouds

Light and fluffy like clouds, these meringues are topped with a sweet, creamy topping and fresh strawberries.

10

What you need:

4 egg whites
1½ cups superfine sugar
2 tsp white wine vinegar
2 tsp cornstarch
1¼ cups heavy cream
¼ cup confectioners' sugar
1 tsp vanilla extract
1 lb/450 g strawberries, hulled and halved if large

1. Preheat the oven to 350°F/180°C. Place a round cutter on top of a sheet of parchment paper and carefully trace around it with a pencil. Draw 5 circles on 1 sheet and repeat on another sheet, so you have 10 circles. Put the parchment paper, drawn-side down, on the baking sheets.

2. Put the egg whites in a large bowl, then beat, using an electric handheld mixer, until the egg whites stand in firm, stiff peaks.

3. Beat in the superfine sugar a tablespoonful at a time until the mixture is shiny and stiff, then beat in the vinegar and cornstarch.

4. Spoon the mixture onto the circles on the parchment paper and make a dip in the center of each with the back of the spoon.

5. Bake for 10 minutes, then turn the oven down to 250°F/120°C and cook for 1 hour. Remove from the oven and let the meringues cool a little, then move to a wire rack.

6. Beat together the cream, confectioners' sugar, and vanilla extract in another large bowl until the mixture stands in soft peaks. Spoon the cream into the dips in the meringues and top with the strawberries.

Step 3

Step 4

Step 6

My Own Apple Pie

Make apple pies that are extra special by cutting out your initials and adding them to the top of each pie.

10

* plus chilling time

What you need:

1¾ cups all-purpose flour, sifted

pinch of salt

2 tbsp confectioners' sugar

½ cup cold unsalted butter, cut into small pieces

1 egg, separated

1–2 tbsp cold water

Filling:

6½ cups, peeled, cored, and thinly sliced baking apples

2 tbsp orange juice

1 tsp ground cinnamon

3 tbsp superfine sugar

1. Put the flour, salt, and confectioners' sugar in a medium bowl and mix together. Rub in the butter, using your fingertips, to make a soft mixture.

2. Stir in the egg yolk and water, using a wooden spoon, then bring the mixture together with your hands to make a dough. Cover with plastic wrap and chill in the refrigerator for 30 minutes.

3. For the filling, mix the apple with the orange juice, cinnamon, and superfine sugar.

(!) 4. Preheat the oven to 400°F/200°C. Divide the apple mixture between 4 ramekins or other small heatproof dishes. Wet the rim of each dish.

(!) 5. Roll out the dough and cut out 4 round tops. Top each pie with a round, trim the edges, and crimp the edges with a fork.

(!) 6. Roll out the remaining dough and cut out letters of your choice. Brush each pie with egg white and place the letters on top. Make a slit in the top of each pie, brush with more egg and put on a baking sheet and bake for 30–35 minutes until golden brown.

Raspberry Parfaits

These pretty gelatins are so yummy they would be good on their own, but when topped with custard and sprinkles, they are simply delicious!

10

* plus chilling time

What you need:

1 package raspberry gelatin

1¼ cup fresh raspberries (reserve a few to decorate)

sprinkles, to decorate

Cream:

scant 1 cup heavy cream

2 egg yolks

1 tsp cornstarach

1 tsp superfine sugar

2 drops vanilla extract

1. Make the gelatin as directed on the package to make 2 cups of liquid gelatin mixture. Divide the raspberries among six 1-cup small heatproof sundae dishes.

2. Pour the liquid gelatin onto the raspberries, dividing it equally among the glasses. Place in the refrigerator for 1–2 hours to set.

3. To make the cream, place the heavy cream in a small saucepan and gradually bring to a boil. In a large heatproof bowl, use a fork to whisk together the egg yolks, cornstarch, sugar, and vanilla extract until smooth.

4. Pour the hot cream onto the egg-and-sugar mixture, whisking all the time with a whisk. Pour the mixture back into the pan and continue whisking over a very gentle heat until it just starts to thicken. Remove from the heat and let cool.

5. Pour the cooled custard onto the set gelatins and decorate with the sprinkles and the remaining raspberries.

Step 3

Step 4

Step 5

Index